Opus 22

Carlo Scarpa
Museo Canoviano, Possagno

Text
Stefan Buzas
Judith Carmel-Arthur

Photographs
Richard Bryant

Edition Axel Menges

Editor: Axel Menges

ISBN 978-3-930698-22-6

2nd, revised edition

Reproductions: Gábor Mocsonoky, Budapest
Printing and binding: Graspo CZ, a. s., Zlín, Czech Republic

Design: Axel Menges
Plans: Roger Thomson, London

Contents

Stefan Buzas and Judith Carmel-Arthur

Canova and Scarpa in Possagno

»The real world is a jumble of awesome complexity and immeasurable charm. Even the inorganic world of rocks and stones is a boundless wonder. Add to that the ingredient of life and the wonder is multiplied beyond imagination ...« (Peter Atkins, *The Periodic Kingdom*)

These sentences, quoted from a scientist's writings, come to mind when confronted with miraculous effects of light and form, be they due to nature's infinite richness, or to the boundless imagination and creative skill of great artists. In the small addition to the Canova Museum in the village of Possagno, lying in the hills near Treviso in the Veneto, the Italian architect Carlo Scarpa exhibited this boundless wonder of light without which neither life nor art could exist.

Scarpa was commissioned in 1955 by the Superintendent of Fine Arts, Venice, to design this small extension to the existing, early-19th-century Canova plaster-cast gallery and to reposition statuary from the museum's overcrowded collections. Completed in 1957, the extension has a timeless and dramatic quality. The Canova Museum was already remarkable in presenting the collective works of a single individual. With the new extension the museum became – at that time – a unique amalgamation of the Neoclassical and the modern, the old and the new, in uncommon harmony. Both Scarpa's addition and the original 1830s galleries are bathed in rays of natural sunlight which animate the agile forms and refined surfaces of Canova's sculpture.

The extension was meant to function in two significant ways. The first was as a timely regional, if not national commemoration of the late-18th-century Italian sculptor, Antonio Canova (1757–1822), born in Possagno and also entombed there in the Neoclassical »Tempio Canoviano« resting on the summit of Possagno's hill. In 1955 the 200th anniversary of Canova's birth was imminent, and a sympathetic enlargement of the rich, but somewhat restricted spaces of the existing plaster-cast gallery was envisaged as an appropriate tribute. Scarpa's extension, in empirical terms, was also founded in the practical necessity of augmenting the permanent exhibition space of the existing galleries, amplifying and rationalising the display of this unrivalled surviving collection. The new extension would exhibit Canova's many original plaster casts – unusual in their raw power which is often lost in the final polished marbles – in addition to a selection of smaller works, preparatory sketches and *modelli* fabricated in terracotta or sculpted of marble, hitherto accommodated largely in storage rooms.

»Classicism favoured nature idealised in antique form rather than nature natural.« (J. Mordant Crook, *The Greek Revival*)

Journeying to the Museo Canoviana is nothing short of a pilgrimage to experience first-hand the most exquisite traditions of Italian design surviving from the distant and more recent past. Travelling in a north-westerly direction away from Venice, minor roads lead through the small town of Castelfranco, then climb onwards towards the pretty hill town of Asolo where cool winds and rich greenery offer summer retreat from the lagooned city. Caressing wooded hills, the winding roads emerge into an open valley. Distant hills suddenly appear towards the north with the higher reaches of the towering Dolomites in the further distance. In the picturesque greenery of the nearer foothills lies, somewhat unexpectedly, the harmonious fabric of a honey-coloured, domed temple bearing the unmistakable profile of the Roman Pantheon. Turning left from Ascolo is the small village of Possagno, within the shadow of Monte Grappa, mostly and sadly remembered for the dreadful battles fought there in 1917 between Italy and the invading armies of Austria.

Entering Possagno, mountains of stacked bricks and clay shards betray the ancient local traditions of earth-bound craftsmanship. An upper road leads to a broad straight avenue projecting upwards as the »backbone« of the Possagno hill. At its peak lies the unusual, domed temple glimpsed earlier from the distance. This Pantheon-like structure is the Tempio Canoviano, begun in 1819 and originally planned as the village's new parish church, but soon chosen as the final resting place of Possagno's most famous son. Its conception and indeed the very intervention of its Neoclassical design into the traditional architectural character of this quiet village were due to Canova himself.

The structure was conceived by Canova, and its construction initiated at his own expense. Incomplete at the time of his death in 1822, the Temple was finished in 1830 under the instruction of his half-brother and sole heir, the Abate Giovanni Battista Sartori (1775 to 1858). The building was a monumental architectural expression of contemporary Neoclassical design, the late-18th-century style which Canova championed and which his sculpture is so often quoted as embodying in its purest sense.

Leaving the Temple, a lively flight of steps descends to a path leading back towards the village. Across the path is an unremarkable, white stucco-rendered house with shuttered windows. Building forms and superbly crafted local materials of wood, stone and terracotta speak of the modest, domestic architectural traditions of the Veneto. Here there is a large and arched stone entrance and, above, a rectangular panel framed by laurel garlands identifies this as the birthplace of Antonio Canova. An additional notice inscribed with large Roman lettering and set between the windows announces the presence of the »Gypsotheca Museo Canoviano«. Enticed through a modest, arched doorway, one enters the long arcaded passageway and inner courtyard, and from there into one of the most subtle and pleasurable museums even in this so art-filled land.

The early history of the museum is instructive. Following Canova's death in 1822, as the sculptor's sole heir Giovanni Battista Sartori had the contents of Canova's vast studio in Rome transported to Possagno. There Canova had also kept a studio at the family home. Together, surviving artefacts from both locations formed the nucleus of the present museum. They included a multitude of plaster casts, unfinished and unsold marble sculptures, *modelli* and sculptural sketches fabricated of terracotta and wax, and a selection of two-dimensional works including drawings, watercolours, and tempera paintings on black ground, in addition to working tools and personal momenti. By 1832 Sartori commissioned the architect Francesco Lazzari to construct a museum on the family's property, adjacent to the house where Canova was born, in order to

1. Antonio Selva, Tempio Canoviano, Possagno, 1819 to 1830. (Photo: Richard Bryant.)

preserve this extraordinary collection. The first plaster-cast gallery was thus accommodated in Lazzari's Neoclassical building completed in 1836, with its tripartite basilica plan, imposing coffered vaults, and large clerestory windows which flood the three interior galleries with an abundance of diffuse light. The first »keeper« of the Canova collections chosen by Sartori was the Possagno sculptor »Tonin« Pasino who bore Canova's own nickname. By 1853 Sartori had also established the predecessor of the present Canova Foundation to which he legally bequeathed his half-brother's immovable assets.

Unfortunately, the present text is not long enough to afford a full examination of the rich potential offered by the collections in the Museo Canoviano. However it is worthwhile offering some observations about the nature of those collections, thus establishing something of a context for further comments. The first of these observations is the often overlooked fact that the act itself of sculpting is a demanding and rigorous physical process; one requiring great precision, strength and manual skill. The sheer physical beauty of Canova's work perhaps all to readily disguises the long hours of labour and technical authority each finished work entailed. Contemporary sculptural procedures were outlined and illustrated by line drawings in the practical handbook, *Istruzione Elementare per gli Studiosi della Scultura*, published by Francesco Carradori in 1802, an invaluable source for understanding Canova's production techniques.

At Possgno, as the museum's catalogue affirms, it is possible to follow the many individual stages of Canova's method, beginning with the choice and use of tools, the drawings or painted preparatory sketches, the making of wax and terracotta sketches in which he first expressed his compositional or figural ideas, and then the full-sized clay models from which the plaster casts were taken, and lastly the creation of the marble statues achieved – in the concluding stages – with the aid of artificial light thrown from candles used to illuminate the many subtleties of surface modulation.

The plaster casts were a crucial moment in this process. They committed the final sculptural idea to a full-scale format. Key points along their three-dimensional surfaces were then marked, or »pointed«, with small nails, and exact measurements taken from between these points and transferred to the marble, allowing studio apprentices to then block out the final figure before Canova himself applied the finishing touches. Several references in Canova's diaries record the number of hours he worked on the originals, and those hours of his assistants in the heavy labour of fixing the plaster casts and carving marble blocks which eventually emerged as the master's finished compositions.

A second observation is that a working sculpture studio in late-18th-century Rome was a site not only of production, but also of consumption. Patrons and potential clients visited the artist's studio to view works in progress and, whilst there, negotiate possible works for the future. The studio also offered a glimpse of smaller works, studies, *modelli* and sketches reflecting the unique processes of artistic invention. Other and perhaps competing patrons' commissions might be glimpsed during execution, spurring desire to engage the master's future services for one's own pleasure and edification. The studio functioned as a sort of showroom of past, present and potential projects, clearly taking on an added »sales« factor.

It is indeed rare in the history of 18th-century sculpture that the contents of such a renowned artist's studio should survive so fully intact. It is due to the vision of Sartori that such a resource remains available to inspire further study not only of Canova, but also of the intricate relationships between sculpted artefacts from the period, processes of their making and the contemporary climate of patronage. The collections at Possagno allow rare insight into the nature of sculpture as a working profession.

But what are some further implications for the museum of Sartori's foresight and generous benefaction? Lying at the heart of his original impulse to preserve Canova's possessions for posterity there is the conception of a »collection« as a »bastion against the deluge of time«.

Sartori's decision to maintain the studio artefacts intact as a group effectively rescued that store of objects from dispersal and possible loss. The act of establishing a permanent collection can be viewed in retrospect as a gesture of salvation – especially of vulnerable smaller modelli and terracotta sketches – from the natural ravages of time and changing tastes.

The museum's collection is not a complete »set« in that it does not provide a definitive *catalogue raisonné*, but it is monographic – that is, of Canova only. By preserving the artefacts of a single artist as a sustained group, and by ensuring their survival under the auspices of a Canova »foundation«, Sartori in effect took it upon himself to »construct« how history – in retrospect – would view his famous half-brother. Posterity largely sees Canova triumphal, as he is presented to us by the museum. As a result of the museum being what and where it is, our perception of Canova is also totalizing. Visiting the museum, we experience him from birth, through life, up to the moment of his death. He is presented to us ready-ordered. But this is not necessarily a criticism. On the contrary, in the end we are invited to travel through the various phases of the artist's life and his career, in consequence coming to know him more deeply, more heroically.

Antonio Canova was born in Possagno on 1 November 1757. Early important sources about him include the first catalogue of his works by Tadini (*Le sculture e le pitture di Antonio Canova pubblicate fino a quest' anno 1795*) published in Venice in 1796. Around the time of Canova's death two further sources were published, one the exhaustive 14 volume catalogue in the form of an opera completa by Teotochi Albrizzi – *Opere di scultura e di plastica di Antonio Canova* (Pisa, 1821–24) and the second the biography by Paravia – *Notizie intorno alla vita di Antonio Canova* (Venice, 1822).

Shortly afterwards, Canova's own close friends and associates contributed to the growing eulogies of the artist, including two separate volumes by the Italian historian of sculpture, Count Leopoldo Cicognara – *Biografia di Antonio Canova* (Venice, 1823); *Storia della scultura dal suo risorgimento in Italia fino al secolo di Canova* (Prato, 1824) and the influential volume by the French theorist and historian Quatremère de Quincy – *Canova et ses ouvrages* (Paris, 1834). Such sumptuous *compendia*, some including expensive line engravings of the works, published so shortly after the artist's death attest to the high cultural significance Canova was already seen to have attained.

Canova's life offers a biography ruled by an exuberant desire to create, although its details are relatively simple ones. To list, to describe and to evaluate his vast number of sculptures – including some 60 portrait busts close on 40 statues, and over a dozen figural groups – is beyond the scope of this text which intends only to tell his story in abbreviated form. Even this modest account, however, easily betrays the rapid progress towards critical recognition which his talent came to enjoy.

Canova's father, Pietro, was a local stonemason of some repute who died in 1761 when the young Antonio was just 3 years old. One year later his mother married Francesco Sartori of the neighbouring village of Crespano, leaving her first son to be raised in Possagno by his paternal grandfather Passino, also a stonemason and sculptor of modest religious monuments. Her son by this second marriage was Giovanni Battista Sartori, Canova's half-brother, lifelong friend and the sole executor of his estate.

Canova's grandfather may have been the first to detect the child's unusual natural affinity to stone. By the early 1770s Canova had left Possagno for Venice where he would receive a traditional artistic education, and where his pronounced natural ability would first win favour within the ranks of the patriciate. He was apprenticed to the sculptor Giuseppe Bernardini, but was later present in the workshop of the sculptor Giovanni Ferrari. He is known to have carefully studied works in the collections of the Accademia, often drawing there, and perhaps more significantly to have often studied the well-known plaster casts after the antique in the famous collection of Filippo Farsetti. Goethe had visited that collection in the 1770s, and admired it as one of the most comprehensive of the latter 18th century.

At this time, such collections of plaster-cast replicas after celebrated antique originals remained largely in private hands. But permission could be obtained, as Canova did, to study them by freely sketching and making carefully measured drawings. By the late 1700s, cast galleries had become more important than ever in the training of future artists. They encouraged methodical stylistic analysis, and remained a main source for study of the human figure in action and repose. They were also the most valuable available source for promoting knowledge of classical statuary, busts and reliefs. For Canova, the Farsetti collection was an invaluable early source, equivalent in its impact upon him to the sculpture collections of Rome which he would later study.

The patronage network to which he gained access in Venice can equally not be underestimated. Canova subsequently produced a significant tomb monument for Pope Clement XIII, cousin of the Farsetti family. Some of his earliest works in marble were already recognised for their technical virtuosity, such as the two *Baskets of Fruit* of 1774 now in the Museo Correr which were given pride of place along the landing of Farsetti's Venetian palace. A terracotta copy, now in the Accademia in Venice, of Farsetti's plaster cast of the acclaimed antique *Wrestlers* amongst the collection of the Tribuna of the Uffizi Gallery, Florence, then won for Canova a prestigious 2nd prize at the Accademia. These were the first indications of the great works to come, and the type of patronage network in which Canova would rapidly become a major player. Few artists would express themselves in such an explosion of creativity in a succession of great commissions.

Canova went on to produce a series of important figural commissions through the 1770s, being nominated for membership in the Accademia by 1779. His key early works, such as the individual stone figures of *Orpheus and Eurydice* (both 1775–77) and the marble composition of *Daedalus and Icarus* (1778/79) show exceptional maturity and the young master's rapid stylistic evolution away from a vigorous, late-Baroque manner towards more reticent and complex compositions informed by his study of the antique. His work also began to show a more mature play of contrasts between Venetian naturalism and classical idealization.

»As men cannot rise above their principles, so the artists of Greece never rose above the religious and moral sentiments of the age. Their Ideal was that of youth, grace and beauty, thought, dignity and power. Form consequently, as the expression of Mind, was what they chiefly aimed at, and in this way they reached perfection ...« (Lord Lindsay, *Sketches in the History of Christian Art*, 3 vols, London, 1947, I, pp. XIV–XV.)

By the autumn of 1779, Canova was in Rome, intending the visit to be a study of masterpieces of the past. His own record of his travels, and his first impressions of the city are found in his *I Quaderni di Viaggio, 1779–1780* (Venice, 1959). He went on to visit Naples, and the recent excavations at Herculaneum (from 1739) and Pompeii (from 1748), as well as Paestum, Caserta and Charles III's new museum for antiquities at Portici (1750). The figurative frescoes of Pompeii became a lasting inspiration for painterly diversions throughout his life. But it was Rome, with its confluence of artists from the many centres of Europe, which gave him firm understanding and true empathy with art of the classical past.

By the late 18th century Rome was an obligatory pilgrimage for any serious aspiring artist. This was the city »where it is hardly to be believed what is constantly being found in Rome and its surroundings, for barely a day passes without one coming across a statue, a cameo, an engraved stone, a precious piece of marble ...« (Anatole de Montaiglon, ed., *Correspondance*, 18 vols, Paris 1887–1912, VIII, p. 324.) This was the age of the Grand Tour. Celebrated antiquities located in and around the city had become a glowing presence in the minds of Europe's elite, educated and wealthy arbiters of taste. What is more, knowledge of the ancients was a kind of nourishment to contemporary culture, and was virtually a pre-requisite for modernity in the arts.

Such knowledge was best acquired first-hand through studying the city's famous artefacts, as Canova set himself to do. But much was also to be gained through brushing shoulders with Rome's community of artists, connoisseurs and archaeological scholars who themselves possessed or had access to the city's acclaimed sculpture collections. These included Canova's subsequent associates, the British archaeologist and art dealer Gavin Hamilton (1723–1798), and the British collector Sir William Hamilton (1730–1803), both of whom shared Canova's passion for the antique and his sensibility for the emerging style of Neoclassicism.

However, it was the antiquaries resident in Rome, notably Johann Joachim Winckelmann (1717–1768), librarian to renowned antiquities collector Cardinal Alessandro Albani, who devoted genuine scholarship to the study of the antique. Under Winckelmann's immense influence, an understanding of classical Greek art was placed on firmer archaeological footing for the first time, while appreciation of the classical past increasingly looked to Greek statuary to reveal inspiration for essential human values of beauty, truth, and liberty – values already heralded by the age of the Enlightenment. Winckelmann's claim that the emerging »Neoclassical« ideal of beauty was one of »noble grace and quiet grandeur«, aligned Neoclassicism with the perceived delicacy and *finesse* of Greek statuary, rather Roman, and carried inestimable authority for young artists such as Canova.

When Canova later journeyed to London, he especially marvelled at the exquisite statuary from the Parthenon in Athens. The Elgin Marbles are that much more remarkable in their superb treatment for having originally comprised nearly fifty separate figures, some of colossal scale, others over life-size. They were originally positioned in the temple's metopes and pediments, well above eye level, and therefore viewed not straight-on, but from an oblique angle well below. Canova wrote to his friend Quatremere de Quincy on 9 November 1815 »... Here I am in London, dear and best friend, a wonderful city ... I have seen the marbles arrived from Greece. Of the basreliefs we had some idea from engravings, but of the full colossal figures, in which an artist can display his whole power and science, we have known nothing ... The figures of Phidias are all real and living flesh, that is to say, are beautiful nature itself.« What Canova so potently recognised in the Elgin Marbles only confirmed the realisation of his youth, that »living flesh, beautiful nature itself« was to be his life's aim, and that these qualities, through his prodigious talent could be realised through the grandiose language of the classical tradition.

But the »true style« of Neoclassicism, so-called by its most ardent defenders in Rome, was essentially a backlash against the exuberance of the Baroque. And the term »Neoclassicism«, coined in the mid-19th century, is difficult to define and remains something of a misnomer or – in the least – a debatable descriptive reference. Broadly speaking, the style was at the very heart of a new apparatus of taste. It was a synthesis of intellectual classicism with romantic naturalism, adding to these a genuine interest in recent archaeological discoveries which empirically demonstrated what was classically »correct«.

Neoclassicism, nonetheless, quickly became associated with mere stylism and more with modish decoration than with the aspirational »new Renaissance« so ardently embraced by its purist advocates, including the young Antonio Canova. In the same sense, Canova's sculptures represent far more within the history of sculpture than his original great fame – as a »Neoclassical« artist – alone could do. For Canova, his presence in Rome was nothing less than a dynamic engagement with the most influential artistic and theoretical developments of his day, and it was the richness of this experience coupled with his intrinsic gifts which led him to be far more than a mere imitator after the antique.

Canova remained in Rome, and by the early 1780s began to produce more mature and sophisticated compositions. The artefacts in the Gypsoteca Canoviano provide an excellent representative chronology of this aesthetic development. Although the museum contains mainly preparatory works, with comparatively few finished marbles, it remains possible to map the highlights of his œuvre by reviewing the collections.

In Rome, Canova began to design a series of innovative funerary monuments which progressively employed less robust, quieter and more sacramental imagery than their late-Baroque precedents. These works also expressed Winckelmann's new ideals of quiet elegance and repose. They included the monument to Clement XIV; that for Clement XIII; the unexecuted monument to the Venetian painter Titain; and the plaster cast from 1817–22 of Pius VI.

The most important of these grandiose compositions is represented in Possagno by the large-scale plaster cast of 1800 for the funerary monument of Maria Christina of Austria. Here Canova brought about a powerful fusion of bold architectural motifs with the human figure. The radically new compositional scheme, developed from the earlier monument to Titian, focused around the architecture of the tomb itself, its severe pyramidal form rising fatefully upwards behind the figures which are aligned in a processional cortege near the tomb's open door. The figures' gestures are reticent; their idealization learned from classical models.

One of Canova's most delicate, popular and admired subjects was the theme of *Cupid and Psyche*, executed in both single figures and in more technically demanding group compositions from the mid-1780s. As much as anything, his work in the genre established him as the 18th-century's master of this erotic-mythological category. At Possagno there is a fine terracotta sketch of 1787 for the famous finished marbles representing reclining figures of *Amor and Psyche* in the Hermitage. There is also a plaster cast dating from around 1800 of a standing *Cupid and Psyche* group. This work already shows the complex intermingling of form and a relaxed sensuality of individual gestures. Although the cast in dicates only one of Canova's formulations of this subject, the Neoclassical ideal of sensuality, lightness and graceful charm is wholly personified in the daring yet balletic pose of the nude adolescent male, a tangible realisation of Winckelmann's aesthetic maxims. Other works at Possagno within this genre include the complex plaster cast of 1789 representing *Adone Wreathed by Venus*, and the standing group of *Venus and Ado*.

As Canova continued to explore the expressive potential inherent in classical subjects, he also refined his interest in themes of masculine strength and pugilism, exploring tensions between irrational Dionysian forces and rational Apollonian virtue. During much of his life commissions for over life-size mythological figures added to his fame and popularity. Works of this type show Canova's mastery in acknowledging precedent, such as that of the celebrated antique *Farnese Hercules*. Sculptors through history have consciously looked to sculpture of the past in order to determine their own boundaries. Sculpture references sculpture, and Canova's approach was no different. But while displaying erudition, he was equally concerned to reinterpret psychological states of turmoil with a new heroic restraint which was completely modern, original, and artistically challenging. At Possagno, works of this type include the statue of the pugilist Damoxenos, and the remarkable plaster cast dating from 1795 to 1815 of the over life-size mythological group of *Hercules and Licus* with its complex triangular outline, a work of exceptionally subtle impact.

Other works surviving at Possagno represent Canova's gifts as a portraitist. Especially after the turn of the century his portrait sculpture gained considerable praise, and was sought after in many European courts. Far more commissions were proposed than could be attempted or completed, and much survives executed in both marble and plaster cast. Canova had the rare ability to model facial character and drapery with an alluring naturalism, but at the same time moderating this with a compositional formality rooted in antique Roman portraiture.

Canova accepted a number of important commissions for allegorical-cum-portrait sculpture, producing some exemplary large-scale statues which prove his ability to reinterpret antique prototypes in a modern idiom. Amongst the works surviving at Possagno are the plaster cast of the imposing figure of *Madame Mère, Leitzia Ramolino*, Napoleon's mother, the original marble now in the Duke of Devonshire's collection at Chatsworth in Derbyshire. In this case the antiquel formulae for sovereign power – a hierarchical depiction of Emperor or Empress presiding rigidly upright and frontal – has been mediated by the feigned grace and languidness of contemporary taste. Canova's statuary responded to the politics of patronage on this and many other occasions.

Canova also designed a number of reclining figures mimicking, while not reproducing antique prototypes. Further, his large scale, heroic statuary was perhaps less portraiture strictly speaking than an exercise in satisfying the market for political memorials. There are several excellent preparatory works for this type of statuary at Possagno, including the plaster model depicting George Washington enthroned in the antique manner of a lawmaker.

One must not omit the considerable number of marble and cast-plaster compositions in bas-relief when recounting Canova's œuvre. Produced from the late 1780s onward, many surviving at Possagno, these works are in some respects closer to painting than sculpture. They emphasise Canova's exploration of purely sculptural relationships between figure and background, as well as his continuing interest in the potential of sculpture to tell a story. Drawing their abundant subjects from Greek mythology and tragedy, as well as from the Old and New Testaments, their format is based upon the conventional geometry of antique, primarily Attic Greek stelae. In Canova's hands compositions such the bas-relief for Nicola Antonio Giustiniani became exceptionally lively and powerful.

Amongst the more than one dozen sculpted figural groups executed by Canova, *The Three Graces* exemplifies his deep understanding of the human body and its infinite subtleties of movement. Carved for the Empress Josephine, it is perhaps the most famous of his works. Such creations belie the often held opinion that the Neoclassical vision of Canova could be cold, its intentions merely »skin deep«. Canova's treatment of the theme is anything but impersonal. The graceful intertwining of figures in this revolving composition shows the delicacy with which Canova was able to interlock apparently living forms in contrapuntal harmony. The ef-

2. Antonio Canova, *The Three Graces*, 1813–16. (Photo: Richard Bryant.)

fortless transition between one figure and another absorbs the spectator, drawing the eye into the deceptive simplicity of the figural group. In his biographical memoir of the sculptor published in 1824, Count Cicognara observed the elegant forms and tender embraces of the figures, and how gently a play of light animates their surfaces.

The plaster-cast for *The Three Graces* now stands superbly positioned in the Scarpa wing of the museum. Its pristine state invites the viewer to contemplate Canova's sensual expression of Winckelmann's maxim of »noble simplicity and quiet grandeur«, and to genuinely appreciate the sentiment and technical virtuosity which produced such sculptural rhythm and figural poise, raising this superbly crafted sculpture into a masterpiece of its period.

During the course of his remarkable career, Canova had periodically journeyed to Possagno. Towards the end of his life, suffering chronic illness, he finally returned there, devoting the last years of his life to the design and construction of the noble Neoclassical-style Temple. Construction began under the supervision of the architect Antonio Selva, and Canova himself laid the foundation stone in an elaborate ceremony on 11 July 1819. Within the church there is Canova's last major work.

A year before his death he was engaged on a large funerary monument dedicated to the Marchese di Salza, but little could he have known that his own funerary monument would shortly be constructed from this unfinished composition, and would shelter his own body and that of his half-brother. Antonio Canova died on 13 October 1822. At the time of his death in 1822 no living sculptor in Europe could command the immense admiration, and sometimes disparagement, which Canova had received during the course of his lifetime.

Having attempted to describe the remarkable talent, vision and knowledge of one exceptional man, it is now necessary to try to define the rare creative gifts of another, equally exceptional man. But as much as any true architect, because Carlo Scarpa's creativity sprang from his personal response to the subtle variables of light and spatial interplay, no publication can satisfactorily represent the indefinable balance he was able to achieve between dark and light, void and solid, volume and mass. It is almost impossible to transmit such values effectively in words.

Even the finest of Scarpa's compositions can only remain pleasurable, long after, to the viewer who is intimately and subconsciously aware of Scarpa's fusion of space and the object with light. To convey the magical qualities of his work, even the mythical power of the written word can only give some modest revelation. Richard Bryant's photographs included here come nearest to revealing Scarpa's personal world of intense beauty.

Scarpa's ways of working were perhaps nearer those of architects from past centuries. He did not require either the technical facilities or the fast-paced, professionally organised routine which we so readily associate with architectural practice in the present day. His designs – of which there remains an archive of over 18,000 drawings – were largely executed during the quiet hours of the night, while daytime was reserved for the pleasurable activities of reading and looking, and enjoying a constant discourse with friends and associates. Young and not so young colleagues joined him from many countries to benefit from his cultured approach, and assisted in executing drawings for the realisation of his designs. But in the end there has never been any question that all Scarpa's designs were his and his alone. For Scarpa was renowned for his intuitive skills in transforming through drawing any idea into living matter. The nearest one can come to understanding the complex inception and development of his ideas is to study those drawings.

A native Venetian, Scarpa was born in 1906. The impact of the place of his birth on the manner in which he conceived of architecture cannot be underestimated. By self-definition a craftsman, a problem solver and a maker of interventions in the built environment, Scarpa saw inert form as being infused with life through its discreet dialogues with materials, space, and above all light and time. For Scarpa, the changing shape of light creates the shape of things. Shifting intensities of volume, mass, texture and colour are dependent upon the resonances of light, and materiality is achieved alongside the ephemeral and the transparent. There is a Venetian pedigree to these empowered notions of light, time and transformation, and this pedigree is ever present in Scarpa's Œuvre.

It is possible here only to briefly summarise Scarpa's career with a focus upon some of those moments which contributed most to his eminent achievements at Possagno between 1955 and 1957. Scarpa initially trained at the renowned Accademia di Belle Arti in Venice in architectural design. Although he never obtained his licence, he enjoyed a lengthy and influential teaching career from 1926 at Venice's Istituto Universitario di Architettura, eventually obtaining the distinction of professor. Beginning in the following year he worked as a professional designer, and continued to run a design studio through the early 1960s.

In 1927 Scarpa obtained the prestigious post of artistic consultant to the Murano glass manufacturer Capellini, subsequently taking up a post of the same title with the famous Venini firm on Murano in 1933 and remaining there until 1947. Scarpa's formative designs for Venini glass already effortlessly showed his unique facility for invention, along with his abiding regard for long-established artisinal tradition.

From the beginning, Scarpa maintained a progressive dialogue between crafts conventions and the disciplines of design. His experimental approach sought out the innumerable possibilities offered by materials and methods, and he spared no effort in liasing closely with master craftsmen and artisans with whom he came to form long-lasting co-operations. Acknowledging his collaborators with the highest praise, Scarpa considered himself one of them – an artisan – and often worked with the same masters over many projects. In this, Scarpa tacitly acknowledged the profession of architecture as one of inter-dependent and inter-disciplinary relations.

His focus on this essential exchange was itself an assertion that traditions of »manual craft« were a decisive element in the designing and making of new architecture. This point of view betrayed an equally auspicious approach to all architecture as an ongoing process of new research into the indivisible pursuits of building craft and design. Scarpa's experiences with glassmaking first at Cappellini and then at Venini in part motivated his enquiries into the potentials and limitations of craft convention, and were subsequently recognised as a seminal influence in his developing focus upon problematic combinations of the old with the new. These considerations were soon combined to form his strategy for any intervention in an historic architectural fabric.

By the end of the 1930s, Scarpa had become involved with the restoration of historic structures. Over the following years he would gain immense critical praise for his rejuvenation of the interiors of historic galleries and museums in Italy, his work commissioned by various institutions concerned with not only progressive design, but also the tourist industry. The first instance of this type of intervention was in the ancient historic fabric of the Ca' Fóscari in Venice, during 1936/37, where Scarpa's endeavours provided evidence of his consummate skill in the manipulation of materials. This commission also proved Scarpa's sensitivity towards designing structure and space while prioritising the contextual importance of historic artefacts on display. He consistently expressed special concern to retain the authenticity and integrity of any structure. He also looked carefully at the more abstract qualities of atmosphere and light in order to retain the timelessness of any historic fabric in which a collection of artefacts was present, achieving an atmospheric intimacy which evoked the past life of the artefacts themselves and their role in the story of a surviving building.

Prior to his work at the Canoviano in Possagno, Scarpa had also gained experience during 1953/54 in designing the museum interior of the Palazzo Abatellis in Palermo, and was subsequently occupied with similar interventions at the Museo Correr in Venice in 1953 to 1960, and at the Fondazione Querini-Stampalia, also in Venice, in 1961–63. In 1964 Scarpa again achieved critical recognition for his redesign at the Museo Civico di Castelvecchio in Verona, a seminal instance in which the institution was sited in a venerable building being reinvented with mindful regard for its unique past.

Throughout the course of his work in the museum and gallery sector, Scarpa's interventions questioned prevailing notions about museum design and also interrogated the time-honoured idea of galleries as otherworldly spaces secreted within venerable structures often lacking sufficient air or natural light. Scarpa's response to the redesign of such interiors simply addressed different challenges. He looked painstakingly at the whole of a site and its available space. He interpreted artefacts themselves as the active agents to be accommodated foremost in any »exhibition« building scheme. Because Scarpa prioritised the requirements of artefacts, his architectural choices facilitated a new, more purely abstract approach to renovation and intervention, and this is seen perhaps above all at Possagno.

Other early considerations which informed Scarpa's eventual work at the Canova Museum were located in his experimental approach to exhibition display. Part of the success and magic of Possagno rests clearly on the nature of his display solutions which drew together in an entirely new and remarkable fashion much of the experience and expertise gained earlier. His career interrupted by the Second World War, during the late 1940's Scarpa began a series of co-operations with the prestigious Venice Biennale, a relationship which served to bring his work in the field of exhibition and display design to the critical attention of an international audience. From 1948 until 1972 he acted as design consultant to the Biennale, contributing to nine Biennali overall, with a number of acclaimed exhibitions, including that for the works of Paul Klee in 1948, the Book Pavilion in 1950 and the Venezuela Pavilion in 1954–56. In addition to permanent museum installations and the redesign of commercial shops and showrooms, such as his now classic design for Olivetti in the Piazza San Marco (1957/58), Scarpa also designed numerous exhibitions outside of Venice, including the exposition of Mondrian's work in Rome in 1956, and the renowned exhibition of original mural paintings, *Frescoes from Florence*, after the great flood of the Arno in 1966. When that exhibition travelled internationally, other countries received their first glimpse of Scarpa's singular genius in contemporary display design.

For Scarpa, exhibitions, particularly those sited in museums, offered far more than a mere occasion to mediate on behalf of collected artefacts in the illustrious warehouses of European culture. Instead, he conceived of an exhibition as an aesthetic thoroughfare in which all elements of visual culture and the built environment were channelled together. As such, each new exhibition offered the designer a chance to personally assess the artefacts through display design, also bringing new and unexpected insight to bear upon the presentation of works to a viewing public.

Scarpa's manner of both museum and exhibition design drew together various themes. While always acknowledging that environmental design for single and collective artefacts needed to be, certainly in theory, focused upon the immutable factors of space, mass and light, Scarpa equally recognised the same principles as fundamental to architectural expression, and was therefore unforgiving of much traditional museum and gallery design that was not primarily architectural in the first instance. In practical terms, the design of a museum or gallery interior is an intricate affair, requiring refined technical considerations, especially in order to achieve an all-around diffusion of natural light in conventionally top-lit spaces. Scarpa believed the best exhibition designers were those most able to architecturally exploit the complexities of natural light.

To some extent, Scarpa's approach was also an attempt to de-mystify the traditionally reticent museum environment and to provoke a more aware response to the continuum of aesthetic possibilities – past and present – inherent in so many museum settings. To do so he acknowledged the numerous sequences of activities which brought together otherwise separate design possibilities, so that in the end the whole of a building became an exhibit, and a multitude of considerations – structure, volume, colour, and light – were powerfully fused together. In Scarpa's hands, cultural masterpieces assumed a new complexity and their value was renewed, while a building itself could no longer be perceived as inflexible and immune to time, but was rejuvenated by its role in the course of incessant change which he made visible.

The single consistent feature of Scarpa's œuvre which most defies not only analysis, but the power of the written word, is his mastery of light. This mastery was exemplified, above all, in his universally acclaimed eminence in museum and exhibition design. It is therefore appropriate in the present work to celebrate Scarpa's vision by looking closely at one commission in the field of museum and display design which has been consistently heralded in the critical literature as the most

3. Carlo Scarpa, Galleria Nazionale della Sicilia, Palazzo Abatellis, Palermo, 1953/54. (From: Christine Hoh-Slodczyk, *Carlo Scarpa und das Museum*, Berlin, 1987.)
4. Carlo Scarpa, Galleria Fondazione Querini Stampalia, Venice, 1961–63. (From: Christine Hoh-Slodczyk, *Carlo Scarpa und das Museum*, Berlin, 1987.)
5. Carlo Scarpa, Museo Civico di Castelvecchio, Verona, 1956–64. (From: *Global Architecture*, 51.)
6. Carlo Scarpa, Olivetti showroom, Venice, 1957–59. (From: *Global Architecture*, 51.)

outstanding of his masterpieces in this area: the addition he built between 1955 and 1957 in Possagno for the Gipsoteca Canoviana.

In the apparent simplicity of its design, Scarpa's extension at Possagno is both deceptive and ingenious. The existing basilica-like museum was enlarged by a comparatively small addition. Within three distinct and beautifully orchestrated volumes Scarpa was able to create a composition comparable to a musical suite in three movements, also creating a suite in luminosity. It is difficult to describe the abundance of spatial compositions which arise wherever on looks. Suffice it to say that these spaces leave one with a feeling of abundant joy.

The site was originally a narrow, descending plot stretching nearly the entire length of one of the »nave« sides of the existing basilica-like museum. The site thus presented a series of complex variables in respect to both the terrain and the extant structure. Scarpa designed the extension as an irregular »L« shape, consisting of three volumes. The shortest segment of the »L« is attached to the old museum, forming one roughly rectangular gallery along with the cubic »high« gallery. The longest stretch of the »L« is slightly offset from the side of the museum building, running parallel to the larger structure, downwards towards the boundary of the site, and forming an elongated wedge-shaped gallery. Scarpa's design also includes a narrow exterior passageway between the long wedge-shaped gallery and the museum wall. Overall, this arrangement of new, low-lying sequential volumes allows the mass of the 19th-century building to remain dominant and, in comparison, Scarpa's addition is both precious and understated.

Although Scarpa was given complete freedom in the development of his design, and was required to preserve nothing, his plan amounted to a radical modification of the historical site without impeding the integrity of any of the surviving buildings. The new galleries are effectively woven into the original fabric of the site. They are also unobtrusively woven into the existing fabric of the mediaeval hilltown with apparently little effort. Although in part standing free of the museum, the addition is densely packed alongside it and thereby echoes the more traditional associative relationships between generations of existing buildings scattered through in the village.

In addition to the galleries, Scarpa almost imperceptibly added a new boundary wall between the site and the adjacent street. This simple device helped to unobtrusively join his interventions to the local built environment by echoing its own intrinsic irregularity. The wall exemplifies the detailed considerations which Scarpa introduced at every level of his design activity in order to fully integrate the »new« within the urban landscape. The wall also enriches the new gallery wing by articulating Scarpa's interpretation of the traditional walled patio garden as an exterior space both notionally and architecturally integrated with its environment.

Volumetric relationships within Scarpa's design are no less responsive to the problematic site. The new wing is defined by three discrete volumes, each a small gallery. Individually they boast complex relationships with one another, as well as with the existing museum building, the site and the adjacent street.

The exterior of the addition is stucco rendered masonry, with rough concrete finishing around the windows and along the roof line. This quite subtle play of dissimilar surface textures imparts the illusion of change in the perceived scale of separate parts, especially in the juxtaposition of the imposing wall surface with the more delicate detailing around the edges.

The first and largest of these volumes forms a transitional, narrative space between the old and the new. It is a slightly irregular, rectangular gallery with one angled wall, poised immediately off the old museum and the only portion of the new Scarpa wing to be pinned against the original structure.

This top-lit semi-shadowy first area gives a glimpse into the formal arrangement of the lofty basilica. In its centre, Canova's beautiful pyramidal composition representing *Adonis Crowned by Venus* is gently illuminated by a golden-coloured rooflight, this soft source also bestowing an almost tactile quality to the row of female busts. It is also possible from here to look directly into both smaller volumes of the new »L« shaped wing, and forward into the alluring distances of Italian landscape.

This is also the point where all four contrasting spaces meet, tempting one's next direction. With a tantalising view ahead, the second volume begins to reveal itself. This volume is the tall cubic, or »high«, gallery, renowned for its four magnificent corner skylights. To the left down two short flights of steps the third volume comprises the long, wedge-shaped gallery which in its changing levels mirrors the capricious, stepped fall of the natural ridge of the hill as it drops downwards into the rural countryside. At this end of the gallery one comes upon the full-height window that is the one connection with the outside. Here, there is a carefully contrived juxtaposition between architectural structure, sky, trees and Canova's famous group of *The Three Graces*.

Beyond the glazing, the basin of water reflects the sky and supplies a shimmering light from below to counter the strong light from the sky – a memorable invention which imparts a seductive softness to the intertwining forms of *The Three Graces*. In this respect, if in no other, Scarpa was a masterful manipulator of natural light and a descendant of the great Venetian traditions of illumination.

In its blending of old and new, the contemporary with the historic, the first gallery is perhaps the most symbolic. It is the key site in which Scarpa addresses the matter of intervention. Here, along one side of the low-ceilinged room, a former exterior wall of the older museum building is retained and transformed by Scarpa into an exhibition wall for the Canova bas-reliefs. Scarpa also manipulated notions of interior and exterior by creating an »invisible« arcaded passageway down the inside of the wall, alternating the height of the passage with that of the main gallery space, while employing exposed I-beams to form the rhythmic supports of the arcade. Functionally the I-beams mimic classical columns, but their material presence has been made relatively transparent by an overlay of white paint. The meaning of the arcade, however, is not located in the notion of a passageway, but in the positioning of Canova's work along the opposite wall. For a viewer in the gallery, the change of floor level necessitates a pause in motion. The edge of the gallery floor becomes a viewing platform, dictating the most opportune level and distance from which to admire Canova's work. The »invisible« arcade and the viewing platform are architectural devices enabling Scarpa to uncover layers of the building's history in a single narrative moment.

The »invisible« corridor is a primary example at Possagno of how Scarpa experimented with different possible readings of the building as a »container«. Multiple levels of meaning shown in a single architectural moment such as this allowed Scarpa to critically comment on the nature of intervention and to make manifest the principles by which he worked. He is able to offer interpretations in which an historic fabric is veiled or revealed, and to directly address issues of modification and deformation at the same instance in which he preserves a portion of the historic fabric. Slowly journeying through the Possagno galleries, it becomes possible to follow the development of Scarpa's dialogue with the past and to measure such single moments in the story he is telling.

Furthermore, Scarpa's use of monochromatic, white plaster rendering for the interior wall surfaces of this and the other two galleries of the extension was startling in the design of gallery space at that time. The placement of Canova's white plaster and marble artefacts against white walls was a critical response to conventions of sculptural display, while challenging the viewer's perceptions of the subtleties of light, dark and shadow. Scarpa made not only a strongly architectural statement, but one which was perhaps almost painterly in its desire describe in minute detail the subtle transitions of surface volume and texture on both the building and the artefacts.

Scarpa's work at Possagno continues to be regarded as a landmark demonstration of how a highly complex architectural programme involving both the past and the present can be orchestrated. He continues to be admired for his innovations in the overall redesign of the site, down to the most intimate features of the interior. Some of the more subtle features within the galleries, for example, still captivate and marvel, and remain forceful influences of how volumes and artefacts are perceived. Scarpa inserted narrow baseboards of black metal through the new galleries. These radically delineate the junctions between wall and floor, and are unique devices which serve to clarify the individual volumes of the three new galleries, as well as the transitions between them. The baseboards outline the spaces as if by drawn line. In the cubic or »high« gallery Scarpa created a similar effect wherein the surface of the ceiling reaches beyond that of the wall, leaving a narrow inset crevice to fill with shadow, resolutely offsetting the vertical against the horizontal, and causing the ceiling to mysteriously hover.

In its own right, the gallery is a fantastic and lyrical movement in this symphony of light and is a quite remarkable *tour-de-force*. A single step brings one into this enclosed cube, twice the height of the previous space. Such spatial sequence is not unusual. But what is singular, apart from the change in brightness, is the light source. Positioned at each of the upper corners of the cube, four glass rectangles in two matching pairs allow the sky with its moving clouds to illuminate the gleaming white volume of the gallery. The frames of the two longer windows were fabricated from iron, and viewed from the exterior cause the elevation of the stucco-rendered mass to appear changeable. They are supported with slim plaster shelves, bestowing a greater architectonic feeling than apparent in their counterparts. The frames of the smaller cubic windows are obvious only along the vertical contours, while a near invisible triangular member joins the upper glass plate to those at the sides. The result is the entirely unimpeded intrusion of the blue of the Italian sky into the space of the gallery. The surprising, and perhaps even unique invention of the four transparent, inward-penetrating rectangles results in an equally startling condition of natural light.

A normal opening in a wall gives rise to a maximum contrast between the high luminosity of the sky, framed by an almost black edge, to the solid wall surrounding the opening. By inverting this condition and forming transparent membranes of glass, the inward penetration almost totally eliminates harsh contrasts. Surrounding walls are indirectly illuminated, creating a softness that brings the plaster surfaces of Canova's originals to life, caressing the figures. With the sun's rays moving within this luminous cube, angled shafts of sunlight dance along the walls, touching the dramatically placed portrait bust of the sculptor as it is thrust forward on steel brackets, accompanied by a small sketch of Pope Clement XIV below. The whole is an arena of theatrical magic.

The third volume of Scarpa's extension is the »long« or wedge-shaped gallery. Its volume decreases progressively in width as it recedes from the older building, producing a narrow exterior passageway along the wall of the basilica and creating another »spatial« wedge running the length of Scarpa's addition. A glass window-wall of wooden framing comprises that side of the gallery. This simple although radical structural solution within a museum context considerably increases the amount of natural light filling the new gallery, while in part undermining normative interpretations of glass as a mere window onto the outside world. Scarpa not only associates the use of glass with both light and structure, as opposed to view, but employs a contemporary technical solution popularised by the »International« style to express his individual approach to intervention. The window-wall does offer a view, but directly onto the marvellous stuccoed fabric of the 18th-century building. With Scarpa, the window is a vehicle through which to examine an architectural fragment, illuminating a different space, a different time, an earlier part of the same narrative. The new offers a telescopic view of the old, and architecture in Scarpa's hands has ceased to be in any way dispassionate. It is self-explanatory, reflecting back upon itself with celebratory intent.

At the far, narrowest end of the gallery, four floor-to-ceiling glass panels were designed with slim, understated vertical supports giving an unimpeded prospect onto the reflecting pool outside. These glass panels bear framing elements only on the inside, allowing the sides of the gallery to deceptively continue unchecked into exterior space. The implementation of this seamless transition was a critical design statement, provoking free visual play from interior to exterior. The result is a remarkable contrast between textures and volumes, suggesting the apparent ease with which Scarpa could interject changes and juxtapositions in materials and meaning within a single plane. By inverting the concept of »edge«, Scarpa unveiled new architectural and symbolic relations between the inside and the outside of the gallery.

Relationships between the relative heights and depths of the galleries are also defined by the significant architectural detailing of the steps and ceilings. Steps are consistently highlighted as transitional devices, ever leading the spectator into more ethereal worlds. Some are interned by marble sections. All are dramatically undercut, so that the slab stretches outwards horizontally with apparently little or no visible means of support. The most celebrated is the emphatic »floating« step symbolically placed at the entrance to the Scarpa wing. These inventions not only resolve the fundamentally problematic changes of level on the side, but orchestrate the movement of the narrative from old to new.

At Possagno, manipulation of glass by Scarpa was always an emphatic gesture. Glass is present in a selection of sub-narratives, as well as playing a more normative role. It signals the presence of a void, and exacerbates juxtapositions between what is fixed and what is fluid, what is of the present and what endures from the past. It acts as a point of clarification in the observation of Scarpa's design objectives, especially when used as a transparent envelope to intensify perceptions of space and light. The constant movement and mutability of natural light within the galleries also counts amongst the most crucial factors in observing Scarpa's refined positioning of the artefacts.

Scarpa's genius in exhibition design not only exploited his own intrinsic sensibilities, but equally ensued from his recognition of the inherent merits of each work of art. He remained keenly aware of how and where an artefact came into contact with space and light, and designed his means of display around those moments of interaction. Throughout the new galleries the assorted mechanisms of display are invested with diverse measures of reserve. All are poised with self-assurance. Some have a distinctive bearing, while others are entirely more allusive. Whatever their individual character, they offer up solitary stages of the artistic narrative, encouraging a paced, thoughtful journey through the galleries.

One is able to move around displays, getting an intimate sense of sculptural mass and volume. Seductive plays of shadow across solid form become more noticeable, diffuse light illuminates the highly plastic values of the modelling, and profiles are relieved against gradations of light drifting across the background surface of the room. Smaller works have been lifted to a scrupulously judged height. Many are raised upon narrow block stands of polished ebony, its rich dark surface floating against the luminous backdrop of the gallery, the whole effect pulsating in contrasting modulations of light and dark.

Scarpa typically designed each individual stand or platform to perfectly set off a unique artefact, and in reality the props and braces differ markedly in their materials and configurations. Particularly at Possagno the wall-hung exhibits seems to float effortlessly on invisible iron brackets, each strategically placed within a luminous composition of changing light and shadow.

Other supports for smaller statuary are made of masonry, while the large reclining figures are displayed well below eye level on black iron superstructures designed to maintain their weight. The iron and glass vitrines throughout were also designed by Scarpa. Their forms mimic the inward-penetrating lights of the cubic gallery, a delicate black iron armature supporting their floating volumes. They are as transparent as the galleries themselves, and have warranted sustained critical praise.

With Scarpa's interventions, museums also necessarily became centres of contemporary design and as such eclipsed in their possibilities for artistic expression and for learning the more traditional museum enclosure. And all this well before the current emphasis on the so-called »Bilbao phenomenon« gave us museums with »destination« status.

In 1978 Scarpa died in Sendai, Japan. His son Tobia lovingly designed a tomb for his father who was laid to rest at the site of his own architectural *magnum opus*, the Brion Cemetery in San Vito d'Altivole. In *Contemporary World Architecture*, Hugh Pearman wrote, one suspects, with some degree of sentiment that »in the 1970s, it seemed as if one architectural world – the world not only of international modernism, but also of craftsmanship, of conservatism – had died with Scarpa while another world – the world of high-precision, machine-made, radical architecture was taking over«. After setting foot in Possagno, it is impossible to disagree with him.

What is remarkable at Possagno is that the artistic vision of a single architect was so effortlessly able to unite the past with the present, and that the ambiance which resulted intuitively reinforced the aesthetic drama of a valuable corpus of art works. Scarpa's focus on a limited number of materials, perhaps the foremost of these being glass, led to a remarkable uniformity of the structural and aesthetic aims of the project. Possagno has been called one of the 20th Century's finest examples of architectural intervention in an historic fabric. Together with Scarpa's own work at Castelvecchio, it is heralded as less an example of conservation or restoration, than a liberation of architectural meaning and possibility.

During the latter half of the 20th century, increasingly more individuals have journeyed to sites of historic interest, whether they be ancient churches, industrial refurbishments or monuments of rural nostalgia. In the West we suffer an ongoing affair with the historic past. Our passions are, if anything, more acutely engaged after site restoration and conservancy than before.
The more frequently, it seems, older structures are preserved, the more frequently we encourage preservation in some form. We perceive ourselves as enthusiastic participants in the ongoing historical narrative, and remain ever keen to personally experience those parts of the story which came before us. Preservation, restoration, and conservation are all factors in the unveiling of the past, and all continue to enrich contemporary knowledge for the benefit of tomorrow.

What Carlo Scarpa unveiled at Possagno, however, was far greater than a moment of the historic past. His unique and crucial contribution was in formulating architectural metaphors by means of which one could more clearly perceive the dynamic of the narrative itself. By so fluidly juxtaposing the old with the new, he allowed buildings to tell the story of history while being active agents of historical progress at the same time.

In this way his contribution is more full-bodied and fertile than conservation or restoration alone could be. His imagination has adapted the past to the present, reversing the customary approach to the renewal of historic architectural monuments, and in doing so enriching our perceptions of what architecture can be. Especially when designed by such a master.

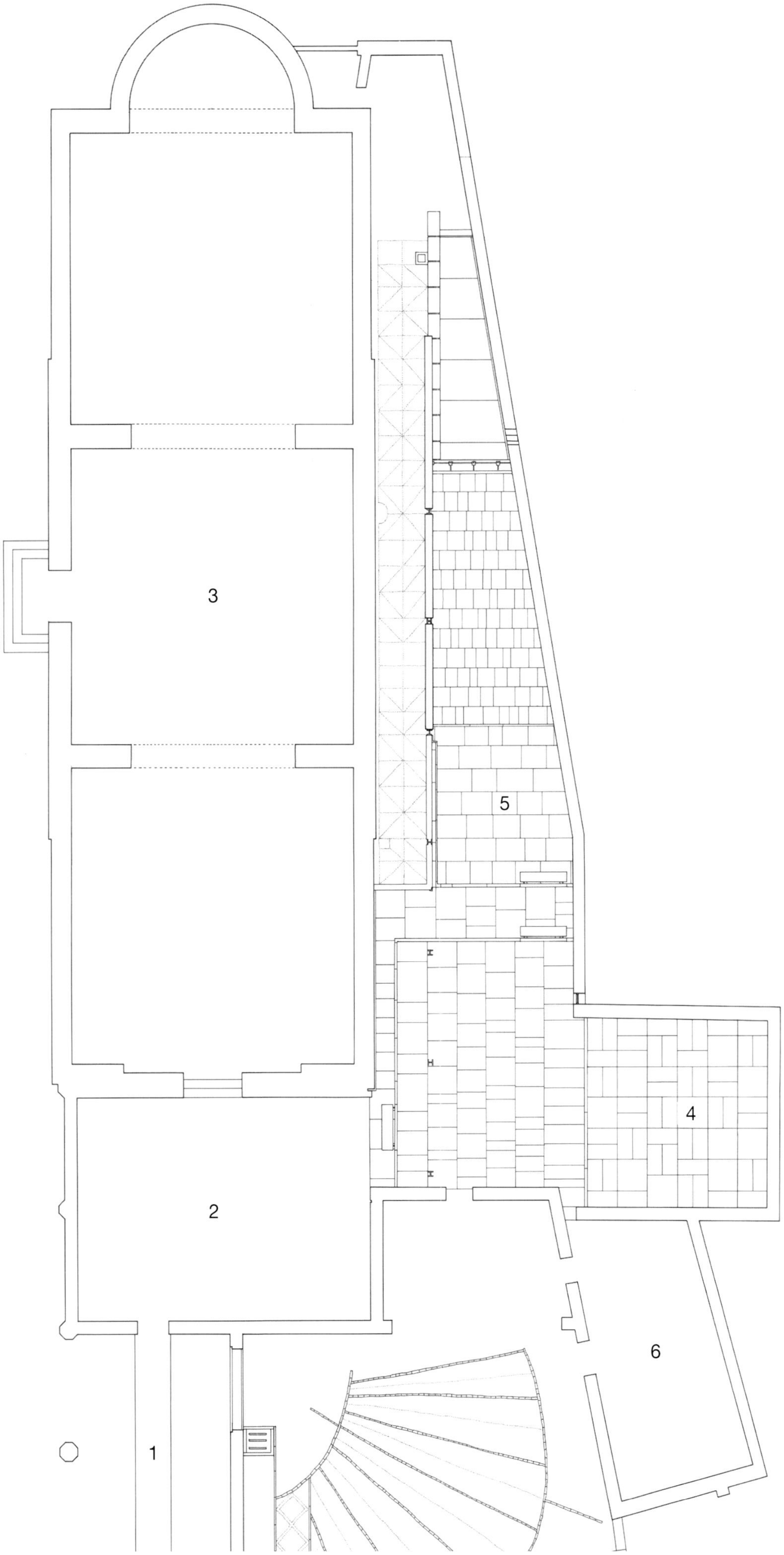
3
5
4
2
6
1

1. Floor plan. Key: 1 arcade, 2 entrance hall, 3 »Basilica«, 4 high gallery, 5 long gallery, 6 the former stables.
2. Reflected ceiling plan.

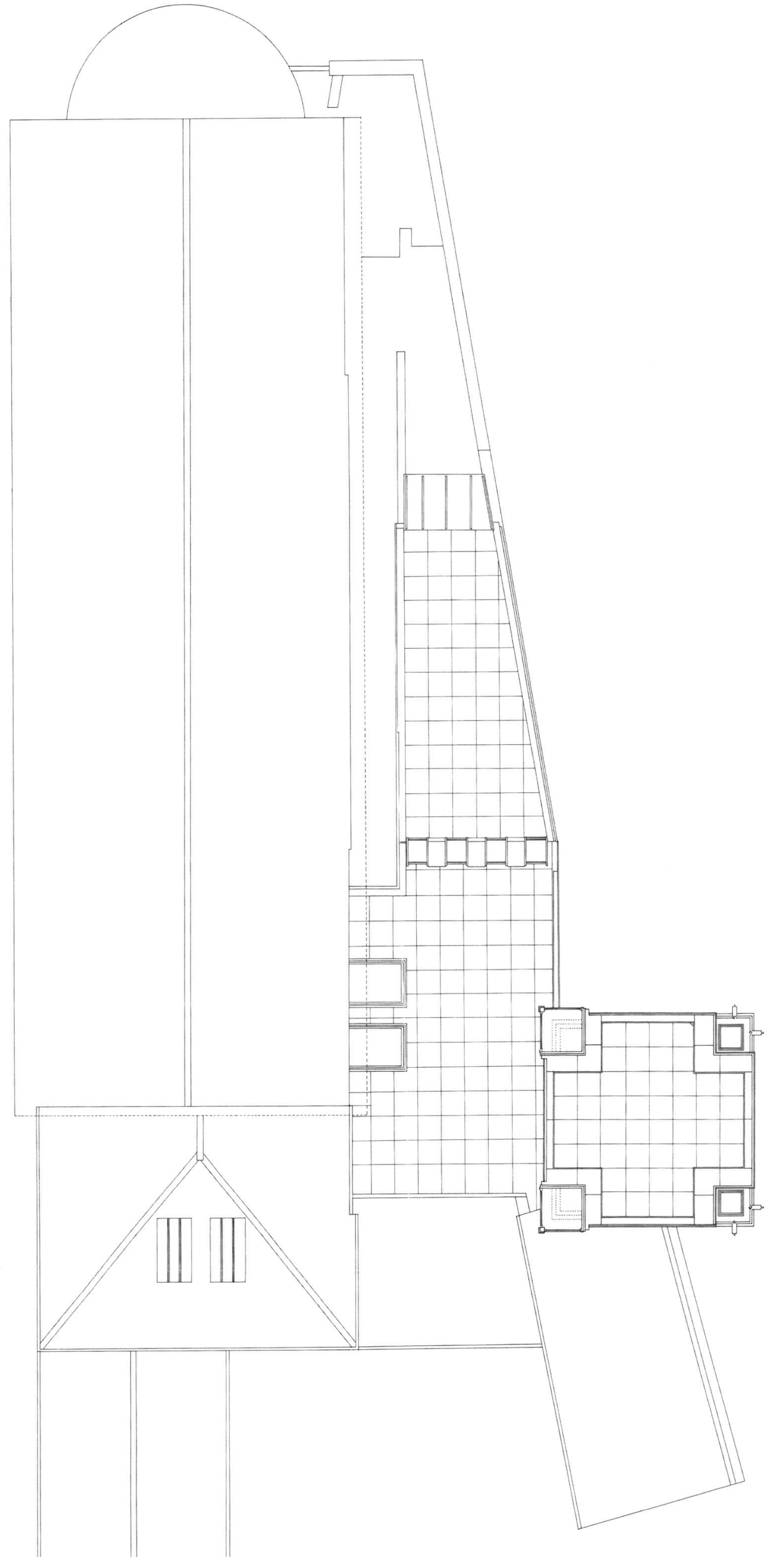

3–6. Cross sections.

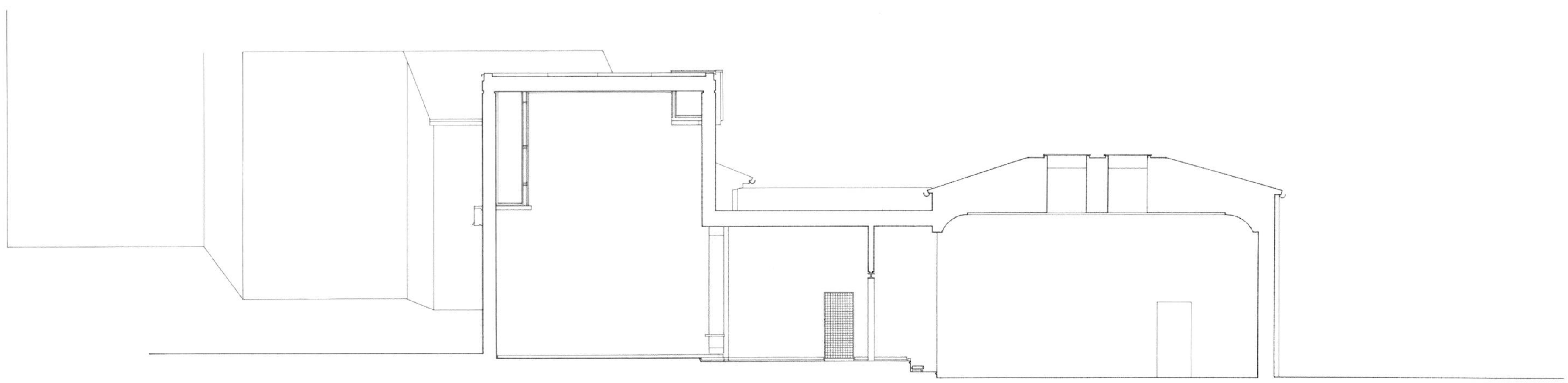

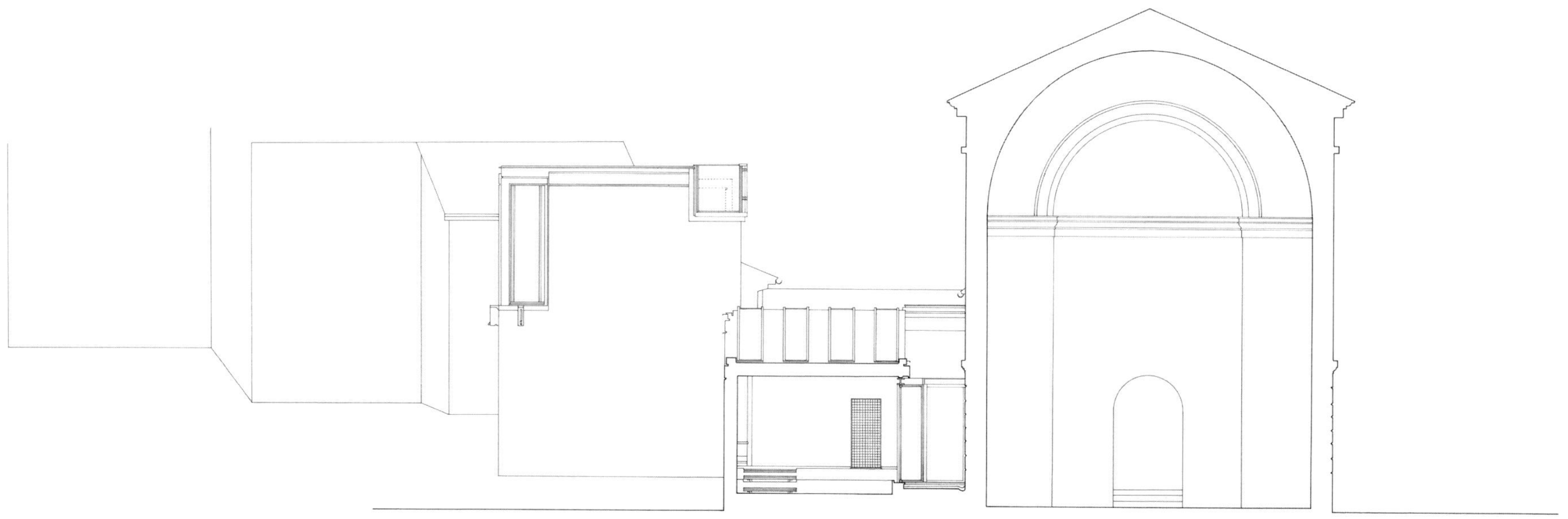

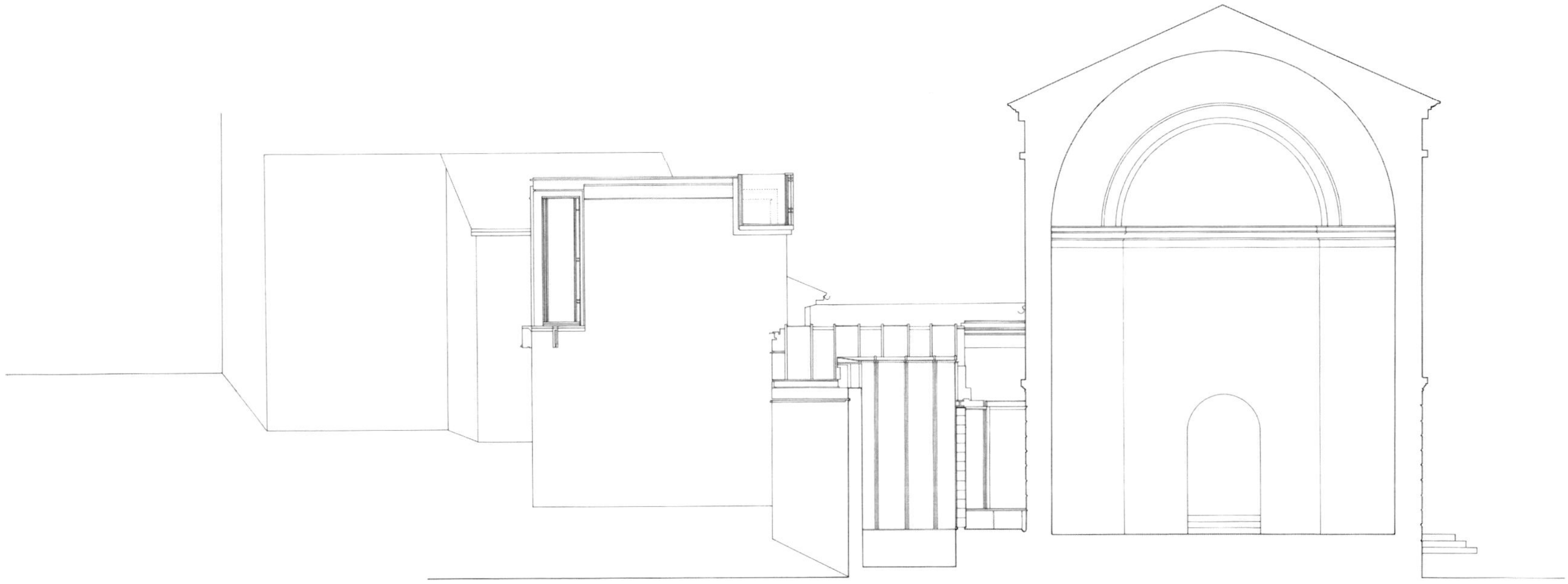

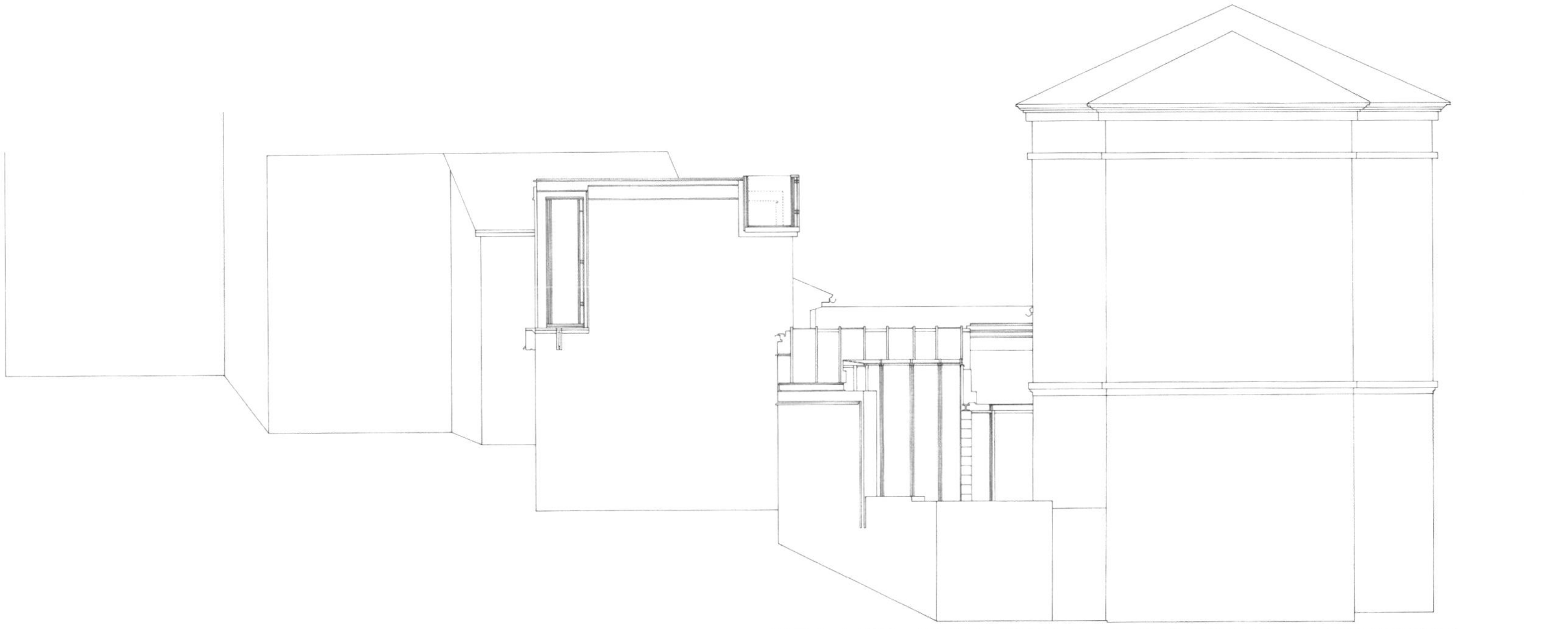

7–10. Longitudinal sections.

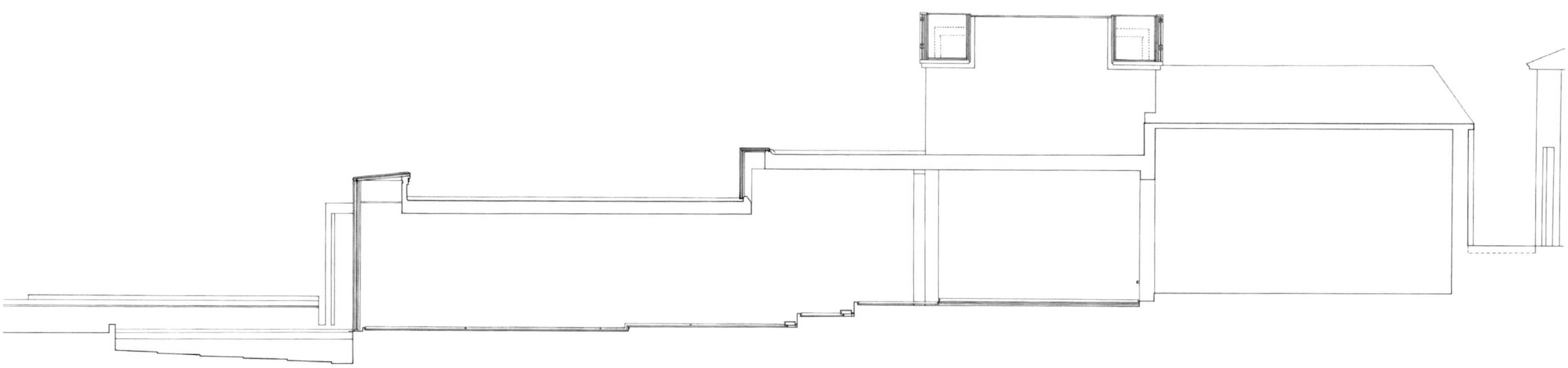

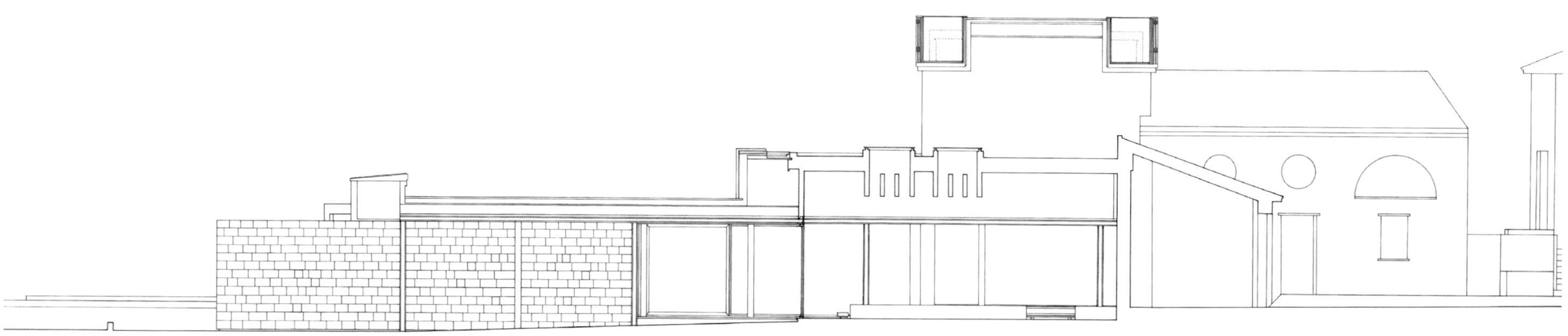

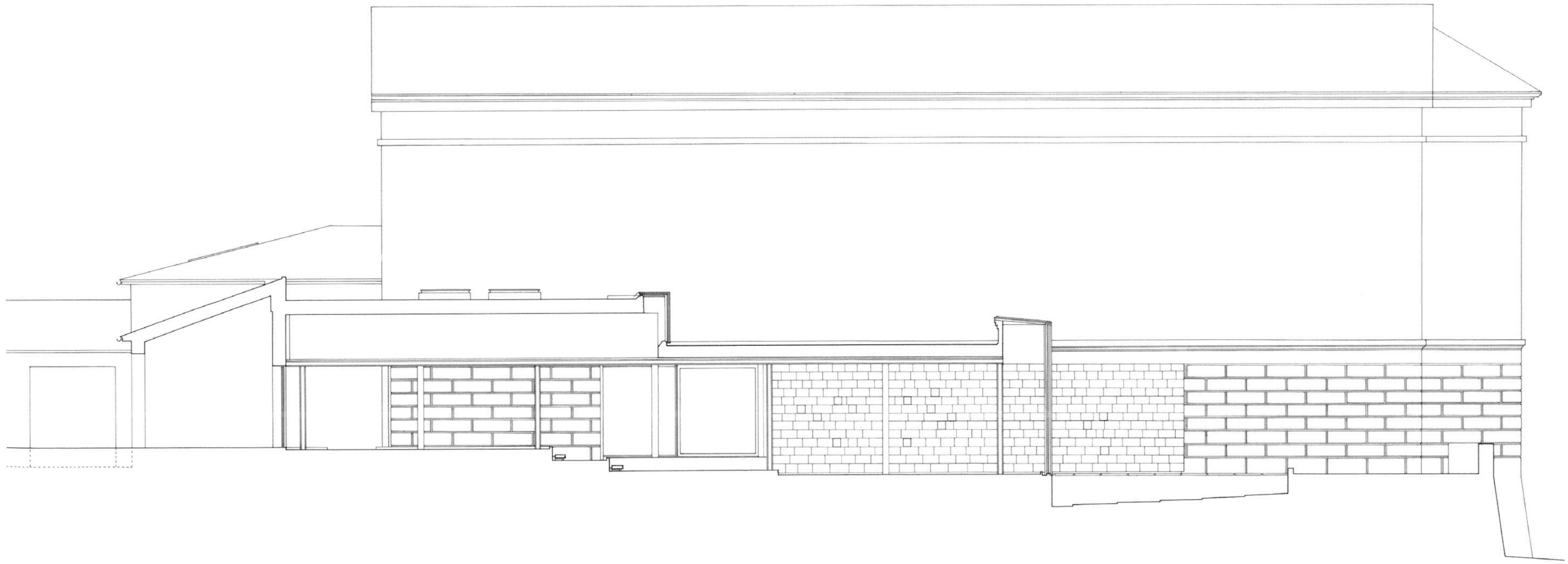

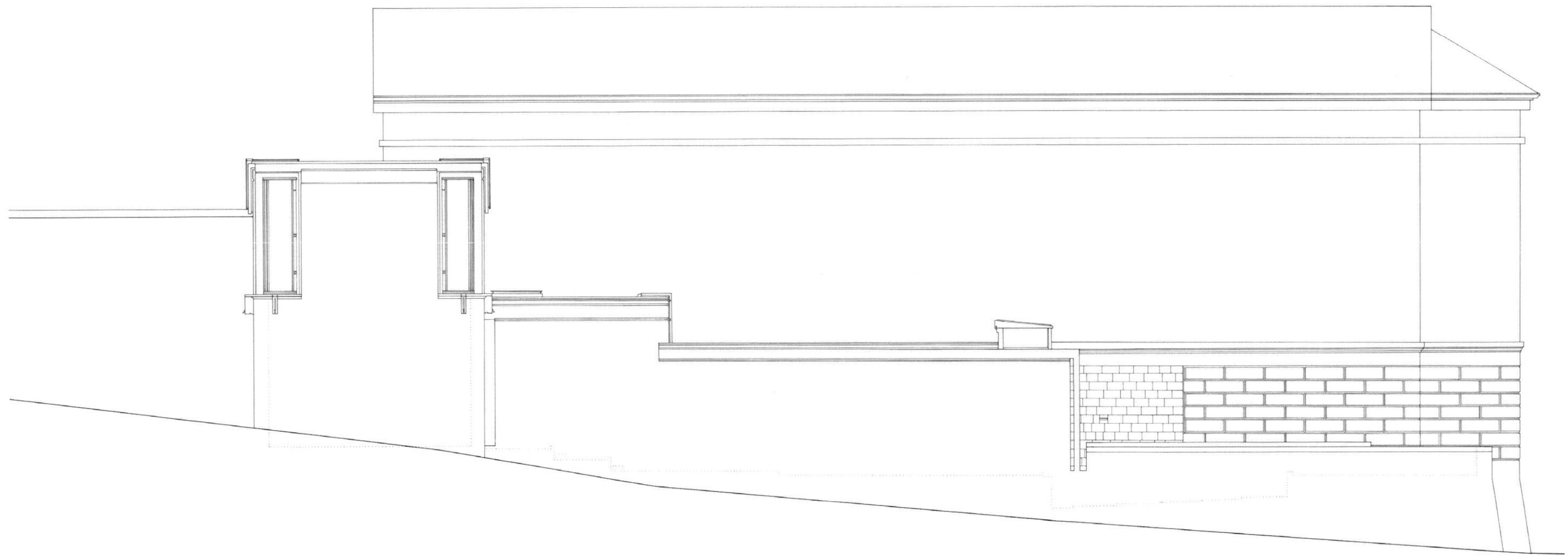

GYPSOTHECA
MUSEO CANOVIANO
QUI NACQUE
ANTONIO CANOVA

1. The entrance to the museum.
2. The arcade with the entrance to the »Basilica« and the Scarpa wing in the background.

3, 4. The entrance hall looking towards the »Basilica«.

5, 6. The »Basilica«.

7, 8. The entrance hall looking towards the Scarpa wing.

9, 10. The high gallery.

11, 12. Detailed views of the high gallery.

13. The four glass rectangles in the high gallery.
14. Detailed view of one of the glass rectangles.

pp. 36/37
15. The long gallery. The high gallery is to the right.

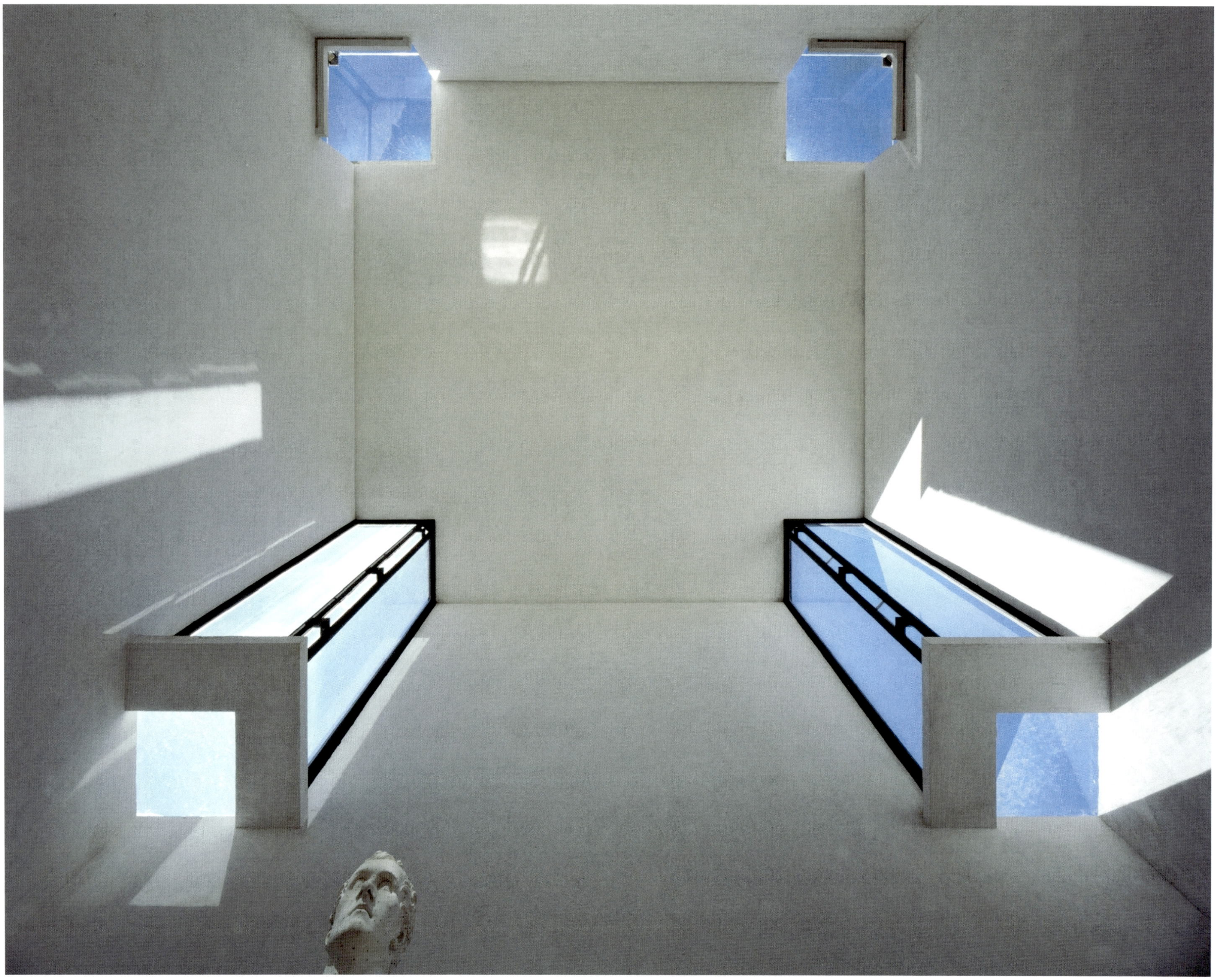

pp. 38, 39
16, 17. Detailed views of the long gallery looking towards its little garden.

18, 19. Detailed views of the long gallery looking back towards the high gallery.

20. View from the high gallery towards the entrance hall.
21. Detailed view of the entrance to the Scarpa wing. The entrance hall is to the right.

pp. 44/45
22. The Scarpa wing looking towards the mountains.

pp. 46, 47
23, 24. Detailed views of the Scarpa wing.

25. View over the roofs of the entrance hall and the arcade towards the high gallery with the pediment of the »Basilica« to the left.
26. Detailed view of one of the high gallery's cubic glass rectangles.

pp. 50, 51
27. View of the high gallery with the former stables to the left.
28. Detailed view of one of the high gallery's tall glass rectangles.

29, 30. The courtyard in front of the former stables.

31, 32. The former stables, now a gallery, looking towards the Scarpa wing.

33. The garden with Canova's house to the right and the »Basilica« to the left.
34. View of Canova's house from the garden.

pp. 58, 59
35, 36. The plaster-cast storeroom in Canova's house.

From left to right: Ivo Zulian, Stefan Buzas, Richard Bryant and Mark Wild in front of Canova's house in 1996.

In the life of a photographer the ideal project comes very rarely. This is the occasion where all the pleasurable parts come together in a dramatic synthesis. Not only the light and ambience, or the intrinsic aesthetic qualities of the subject, but all the other parts of the experience, the local people, the local cuisine, the company, have an influence, and all are so rarely in perfect harmony.

Possagno was such an occasion. The subject matter would have been inspiring enough, but with all the other components it became extraordinary. The alchemic combination of Scarpa and Canova proved to be a potent one. Scarpa's genius for manipulating void and light, combined with the work of Canova resulted in a remarkable architectural gem. The original plaster casts of Canova's great works, which have been kept together and preserved here in Possagno, where the artist lived and worked, have a raw power that is sometimes lost in the highly polished and sophisticated final versions.

My task as a photographer was made much more delightful by the company of my dear friends Stefan Buzas and Mark Wild. Also thanks to Ivo Zulian from the Museo Canoviano, who facilitated all our requests with such good humour.

Richard Bryant